# The Magic Dance

## (Do You Lead, Follow,
## or Get Out of the Way?)

**Jeff Pasquale**

For more information contact us at **www.JeffPasquale.com.**

Editor: Kammy Wood

Cover concept: Maura Pasquale, Vanessa Nicole Ortiz, and Fagaras Codrut Sebastian

Text layout and design: Fagaras Codrut Sebastian

∼

*This book is dedicated to*
*The Rotary Club of West Palm Beach.*
*A terrific group of leaders and first followers.*

∼

*... those desiring a position
above others must speak humbly.
Those desiring to lead must follow.*
– Lao-tzu, *Tao Te Ching*

# Contents

There is an abundance of material on the subject of leadership—what it is, what it isn't, and who is and who isn't qualified to lead. But let's face it, after all of the studies and surveys, it still all comes down to someone's opinion—that person's interpretation of a perfect leader's thoughts, words, and actions.

This is good, because it gives us perspective, which is really how we acquire knowledge and learn to make decisions. Our interpretation of these perspectives gives us a way to view things and to consider who we are and who we intend to become.

So while you're pondering your leadership capabilities, consider this—*maybe the best way to lead is to follow.*

When you boldly decide to go your own way or do your own thing (not in defiance or to make a statement, but for the sheer joy of it), you are either following your bliss, or you're starting a new hobby or business. What determines your success is the amount of passion or energy that's behind your effort.

When others begin to join in or follow what you're doing, you've created a movement.

Said another way, if you have followers, you're a leader.

General George Patton is attributed with saying, "*We herd sheep, we drive cattle, we lead people. Lead me, follow me, or get out of my way.*"

It's safe to say that in order to create or start a movement, three things need to exist—a leader, followers, and those that get out of the way. Simplistic, to be sure, but name one movement that started out as a complex idea.

Allow me to be Zen-like for one moment. Understand that the moment you set out to consciously start a movement is the moment when you will probably be the furthest away from it. In other words, a movement is not something you can consciously control.

People try to start movements all the time with petitions, protests, and YouTube uploads, but at the end of the day, most people are just too busy to get involved unless that movement gains and holds their attention long enough for them to become interested—and then passionate enough about it to join it.

Movements don't usually happen intentionally.

This is not to discourage those of you who are trying to get a business off the ground by creating a marketing campaign (to start a movement) for your product or service. You can do it. Apple did it. Harley-Davidson did it. Starbucks did it.

In each of those cases, the products offered helped to enhance and/or project a lifestyle that the purchaser embraced thoroughly. What's important to note is the history of each of those organizations: from the outset, the founders were really, really passionate about what they were doing; they zealously played their own game, immersed in the freedom to invent, create, and enjoy. They made up their own rules as they went along and were not concerned about securing the good favor of others. It wasn't until their products had attracted an army of ardent followers that a movement was in place.

The good news is: you don't have to create or invent a brilliant new product to succeed. Sometimes you need only to improve upon what's already there. In the cases of Apple, Harley-Davidson, and Starbucks, the founders set out to redefine the nature of an existing product.

Bob Stone, charged with "reinventing government," as part of Vice President Al Gore's team, said it another way—"*Some people look for things that went wrong and try to fix them. I look for things that went right and try to build upon them.*"

*Internal motivation* and *self-satisfaction* are primary ingredients for starting a successful movement.

So far, we've only looked at a movement from a leader's perspective. There is another side to this story—the follower. I recently watched a video narrated by Derek Sivers (author and founder of CD Baby) which introduced the idea that it is the *first follower* who identifies and then causes rapid growth of a movement.

At the time of publication, the video can be found here at Derek's web site— http://sivers.org/ff.

In the video, Derek talks about the shirtless dancing lunatic we see on a hillside amidst a sea of other spectators who are listening to a band play. The guy is truly dancing like no one is watching. After a period of blissful self-indulgence, another person joins in—a follower.

The amazing thing about this video is that the dancing guy is totally unconcerned about whether anyone joins him or not. And that's the central point—he is simply a guy who is passionate about what he is doing, regardless of whether he receives any praise or acknowledgement from anyone else. He just loves what he is doing.

But then the *first follower* comes along. Initially, the follower interacts with the leader—sort of a one-minute bonding experience, so to speak. The follower mimics the leader's moves, high fives him, and encourages him to keep on dancing, and then the follower, too, becomes lost in his passion.

But he does one thing the leader didn't do: he waves to those around him to join in.

Soon, it begins to happen: one by one, two dancers become three, four, and five, —fifteen—and then so many show up that it's impossible to count everyone. The crowd grows to the point where the leader and the *first follower* are no longer visible. A movement has begun.

What suddenly became so attractive about a lone shirtless guy dancing by himself? Once a crowd had formed, that was certainly an attention-getter, but there are a few other things to consider. While what the video presents is not very scientific, it is compelling, because this one person accomplished something that most business owners would kill for—a following.

*If you get no joy out of what you're doing, you'll never attract a diehard first follower.*

From a view of 40,000 feet, there seems to be at least three key components that factor into the shirtless guy's success.

It's important to recognize that his success was in all likelihood never planned or expected. He simply benefited from three simple components that he unknowingly embraced.

First, there was his **inspiration**. He loved what he was doing and he didn't care what other people thought, or who participated or didn't; he was playing by his own rules, dancing to his own beat. (Note that he was also passionate. Passion is extremely contagious when you are having fun.)

Second, he had **visibility**. People could clearly see what he was doing, and they quickly understood what he was doing. No instructions were necessary. He was visibly having fun.

And third, there was **opportunity** for everyone. There was a payoff. People could see the joy that he derived from the experience, and that it was a benefit.

Inspiration was included—they were inspired by his fun approach to the situation. They could see the passion from within that caused other people to participate, simply from emotion; logic was not a factor. In the end, it's important to note that what moved a large number of people to join in was the *first follower*, not the leader.

These three components were the ingredients to his success. While there is no guarantee that you will get the same results by following the same process, it is possible to put yourself into a situation like this, in a business context, and get similar results.

But here's the thing—if you do try to create a movement, you cannot be attached to the results. You must be in the endeavor solely for the sheer joy of doing what you love to do.

It might sound contrived, but you will know if you really, really love what you are doing. If you have a parallel motive for sharing your product, service, or activity with the world, that's fine, but you cannot fake joy and passion for a long period of time and create something meaningful.

If you get no joy out of what you're doing, you'll never attract that critical *first follower*. Internal motivation and self-satisfaction are behind every shirtless dancing guy who is passionate about what he is doing—hobby or not. The real question you probably have at this point is, "Can I really consciously create (and lead) a movement that will benefit me and others, emotionally and financially?"

The answer is yes, but *only* if you find real joy in what you're doing in the first place, and only if your *first follower* is as passionate as you are about what you're doing. How will you know if those ingredients are in place? (See the next chapter.)

The foundation for this whole process of *movement making* is joy. Companies (people) spend millions of dollars on marketing and thousands of hours with test markets, focus groups, and case studies and they can still miss the critical point behind the shirtless dancing guy's success—that he's enjoying every minute of what he's doing.

Which brings us back to the crux of this issue/challenge/phenomenon—it's impossible to fake passion.

Now supposing that your inspiration (passion) is real, there are two other ingredients that must also be at play:

You (or it) must be *visible* and there must be an *opportunity* (or payoff or benefit) that others will get from joining your movement. If your intention is that it's you who ultimately benefits from this movement, it won't be the same. For your passion to be the tipping point, it must be genuine.

The *first follower* can be a challenging concept to understand and accept initially. You won't be going out and recruiting your *first follower*; he or she must be the one who discovers you.

## Considerations

When was the last time you felt joyful (or happy) about a project that you worked on?

———

Were you ever told (or did you ever feel) that you lost track of the other commitments in your life because of a project you were immersed in?

If so, can you notice the difference between when you are fully engaged and happy about what you're doing and when you are simply pushing work out the door?

———

Start forcing yourself to become more and more aware of what makes you happy, inspired, and even joyful. Sometimes we experience these feelings without ever recognizing their appearance or significance.

Inspiration is passion in action.

When you're inspired, you're ready to take action because you are excited not only by the payoff or the chance to see the completion of your inspiration, but you're also excited by the path it has put you on. You're enjoying the journey, as they say.

I'm sure you know inspiration when you see it, but the question is, how often do you actively go looking for it, and what would your life be like if you did? Inspiration is everywhere, but we usually are so self-absorbed or tuned out that we miss 99% of the things that could inspire us. We're too busy being busy.

So take an imaginary picture of yourself right now and take a good hard look at what you see. What are you doing with your life? Work-wise? Relationship-wise? Community-wise?

Are you happy? Are you excited? Are you inspired?

Yes, there are lots of questions, but they are important ones, especially if you intend to start a movement.

Let's assume you are passionate about something—an idea, a product you've just created, whatever. It's there, and it's buzzing in your head night and day. Good.

When that something yanks you out of bed every morning because you absolutely feel that you have to do it, you know you're inspired.

Remember, inspiration is contagious, especially when you're having fun.

I could discuss what to do if you're not excited and inspired, but that's another book. This book is about acting on what you're already excited about.

There is a big difference between being *inspired* and being *inspiring*.

One, you can't be inspiring to anyone else if you're not inspired yourself. I know that sounds a little deep, but it's really quite simple.

Two, you cannot consciously choose to be inspiring.

What to do? Actively look for people and things to be inspired about.

Simple to understand. Hard to do.

This is really a case where you must turn your sights inward and reflect on and respond to what you see going on around you. Sometimes a person or an event will immediately resonate with you and *whala*, you're there. You are inspired. You'll get goose bumps or maybe your eyes will tear up or perhaps you'll just feel good. Whatever just occurred, recognize that it was inspiration.

There will be other times when you are so busy that you won't catch what just happened—and it might not be until the next day or during some quiet time that you'll sit and reflect on it, and *bam!* it hits you—that guy or that event was inspiring.

Once you recognize that you're inspired, at that moment, time stands still. Life looks or feels different in that moment of reflection. And if it's powerful enough, that inspiration will stay with you throughout the day. When that happens, magic happens, because then your inspiration will inspire others who see how it has affected you. Again, you can't force this stuff.

When you practice seeking inspiring people and things, you will find them. We really do get what we focus on. It's like giving you instructions to look for yellow Volkswagens on your way to work. You will be amazed at how many you see, and you'll wonder, *How did that happen?* In actuality, they were always there, you just hadn't tuned your radar to them.

Inspiration works the same way. It can and will happen to you accidentally, with little or no effort on your part, but it can and will happen a lot more if you consciously seek it out.

Let's assume that you're there. You are totally inspired by your project. At this point, you should not even be thinking about letting the rest of the world know. It's your project. Be content to be excited, inspired and consumed by it.

If after three months you're still jazzed or consumed with what you're doing, don't tell anyone yet. What you should allow yourself to become is totally immersed in your project. Let it consume your life a while longer. Allow it to germinate. Don't worry, cool things will happen.

You may soon get so lost in what you love doing that you won't even notice things taking root—the random request to share what you're doing with the media, or the

stranger who hears of your work and wants to learn more.

> *Inspiration is contagious, especially when you're having fun.*

There's something very contagious about inspiration that can never be scripted. Others will be naturally attracted to you when you choose to do cool stuff. But here's the thing—it's never going to be on your timetable, so don't bother setting a completion date.

Focus on what you love to do, not what you're trying to accomplish. It may sound like I'm saying the same thing, but they are two distinctly different intentions. Know the difference. Focus on what you're doing, not what you want.

Yes, this is semantics, but there's also a huge distinction in here. You may be working on this project or thing because there is something you want. But if you are also inspired about what you are doing, strive

INSPIRATION

to focus more on your actions, at this stage of your project, and not the result. In other words, honor your inspiration more than what it is that you want.

Now that you have the passion, the drive, and the inspiration for your movement, you can now consider your visibility and how it can positively influence the movement or project you're planning. Seeking inspiration is the first step you can take in your quest to start a movement.

## ? INSPIRATION
### Foundational Questions

Are you having fun in life and at work? (Do you work like you don't need the money, do you dance like no one is watching, and do you sing like no one is listening?)

Would you do what you're currently doing for free? (Are you already?)

Do you look forward to getting out of bed each day and jumping into another day's work?

Do you think what you're doing is fun, interesting, and cool?

(NOTE: Ideally, you should be able to answer Yes to all four questions.)

There are two aspects to visibility you must consider in order for your movement to take place:

1. You must be **visible to others**
2. People **must immediately understand what you're doing**

(It's like Web surfing. If they don't quickly get what your web site is all about, they're gone.)

So you're dancing and you're feeling happy. Now here's the big question—Are you dancing in public or in the privacy of your home?

This is the thing. If your inspiration is hidden from others, you'll be stuck in an endless loop; if you're looking to do more with your inspiration, it's time for some visibility.

Also, if you're self-conscious or concerned about how you appear, you're not inspired enough. You're not passionate enough.

When you're inspired, you are enthusiastic, and driven to do what you love, whether a spotlight is on you or not.

Visibility, like inspiration, is also something that must be natural. The best way to describe natural visibility is to point out what constitutes unnatural or contrived visibility. Contrived visibility is billboards, television ads, and spam; it's canned and bombastic and designed for maximum coverage at maximum volume. It irritates 99% of the people who come across it because it's forced.

The natural way to achieve visiblity can indeed be a little contrived, but it starts with your intention to be yourself rather than a showman. You're not trying to get maximum attention; in fact, you're not intending to get attention at all. You are simply sharing.

This sounds contradictory, but you have to split the difference somewhere. I'm not suggesting false humility here. You're sharing for the sake of sharing—there's no spin and there's no expected outcome, it's just sharing.

Being natural is about living life out loud, but it has nothing to do with your volume. It's sort of like living life without curtains on your windows, in a way. So you share your stories and progress on Facebook, or on Twitter, or on your blog or website, wherever you go and with whomever you come across.

Visibility is not only about people seeing you but also about their understanding of what it is that you're doing, and perhaps even why. When you intend to start a movement, and you are inspired, visibility may be hard to accomplish at first because your concern isn't naturally one of communicating. In reality, it's probably the furthest thing from your mind because you're so enthralled with what you're doing.

The best way to address visibility is to keep it simple. Obviously billboards and television are not the way. Actually, what you're looking for is not to attract the masses but to attract that *first follower*. And this is as good a time as any to call attention to this person who will play such a pivotal role in your movement. In fact, your *first follower* will in essence become a partner in your business, whether you pay him or her or not.

Your *first follower* is the one who is taking the biggest risk because he or she runs the risk of aligning with someone (you) who might not be able to deliver the goods, so to speak. But your *first follower* doesn't care because she gets it, she's committed, and has taken that first big step for the entire world to see.

You'll be able to recognize a true *first follower* because she will be unimpressed or unconcerned about you; your *first follower* is there because of *what* you are doing, not who you are.

> *If you're self-conscious or concerned about how you appear, you're not inspired enough. You're not passionate enough.*

The other big role the *first follower* plays is one of an influencer. He or she has the power to coax, cajole, and entice others to join in. Malcolm Gladwell, in his book *The Tipping Point,* defined that person, not surprisingly, as a salesperson, someone with charisma and strong skills of persuasion. Gladwell uses Paul Revere and his famous midnight ride as an example.

Revere, Gladwell informs us, was known by many and therefore had the ability to quickly enroll a large number of people who heard his cries for support. Revere had a counterpart, one William Dawes, who took another route but was unknown to the people he was appealing to, and therefore did not produce as large a result as Revere had from his effort.

The "getting it" part is achieved through simplicity. Whether it's an app or a service or a simple new diet discovery, if your *first follower* and other people get it immediately—that is, they look and they can be immediately enrolled in the process, you've got a potential movement on your hands. (Yes, this is totally unscientific.)

Years ago there was a product on the market that no serious investor or consumer would have bet one dollar on. It was called the Pet Rock. It became a movement, a cult thing really, but it caught on mainly because the *first follower* was a heavy influencer.

Tom Peters, author, speaker, and business consultant, refers to it as good storytelling. Instead of dazzling (or boring) people with data, tell them a good story and they'll be enrolled heart, head, and soul. As Tom says, "*Whoever tells the best story wins.*"

## VISIBILITY
### Foundational Questions

Are you (or your project) visible?

How could you share more about what you are doing?

Will people *get* what you are doing?
If not, why not?

Are you self-conscious about what
you are doing? If so, why?

Opportunity brings your intention to create a movement full circle. There are two components to this important aspect of creating a movement.

First, there must be a *payoff* or benefit to anyone who is considering joining. At this point, it's not about the risk, it's about the benefit.

Next, it must be *inspiring*. This is where the circle connects. Remember, you started off being inspired. You had no intention of inspiring others, though that indeed is what you'll end up doing if you're doing this right, and for the previous right reasons.

The benefit (or the payoff) can be any number of things. It could be a financial gain, it could be the pleasure derived from the activity or the ownership, it could even be the feeling of not being left out; it could be the fun or the thrill of the experience, or it could be two or three of the above. The benefit is not the primary motivator but it is certainly one of them, and it contributes heavily to the commitment process.

When the movement is both *inspiring* and *beneficial*, you have a killer movement on your hands. At that point, all of the logic in the world won't change the fact that people are being influenced on a cerebral and spiritual level that you can't measure and you can't trick them into.

They have been moved from within, moved without any apparent reason, moved to a point where they are ready to join without hesitation. When that happens, it's a very cool thing to see.

You've no doubt felt that way at some point in your life about someone or something. There is that magical point where a person crosses that imaginary line and they go from observer to participant, and it can happen in mere seconds.

Try to recall what it felt like when you made the decision to support a political campaign, or join a civic, environmental, or civil rights movement. You probably jumped right in with both feet, and emotionally and physically committed to do what was necessary to support it.

*When the movement is both inspiring and beneficial, you have a killer movement on your hands.*

Keep in mind there will always be people who don't get it. They can't for the life of them understand what all the fuss is about. There are people who don't understand what all the fuss is about regarding Apple, Harley-Davidson, or Starbucks.

Not everyone will be convinced to join, no matter how great your movement is. But when enough people witness the possible payoff of your movement simply by watching other people, your movement is created, and it blossoms.

The payoff becomes the magical fulcrum that helps others make that leap into joining your movement. That *first follower* is pivotal because if he or she sees that benefit, that ultimate payoff, the odds are that *first follower* will be able to quickly communicate it to others just like Paul Revere did.

Inspiration is the stuff that dreams are made of. When people start sensing how cool it is to be doing what you and your followers are doing (or own what you're selling), people get curious and line up. And then other people will begin joining the line just because there is a line.

Always strive to stay focused on your inspiration, your passion (that's your *payoff*). If you do, and it's visible, there's a good chance that viewers will see and *get* the payoff that you are deriving from your movement.

## OPPORTUNITY
## Foundational Questions

What payoff(s) do you see for yourself regarding the project you want to work on?

What do you think the payoff will be for those who see your work (your project)?

What do you feel will most excite and motivate people who join your movement?

NOTE: These questions actually cross into dangerous territory because there is a fine line between allowing a movement to occur and consciously creating (or contriving) one. As difficult as it may be, try to answer the above questions from the point of view of a third party rather than as the creator of this movement who has a stake in its success. When you answer as the creator, your agenda, your biases, and your wishful thinking will tend to take over, and what appears to be a sincere response is really your ego taking over.

> *Connect, associate, identify, and feel in harmony with your project, your movement, your passion.*

# THE MOVEMENT

**4**

All of the previous pages refer to a movement as a group result or effect, but what's critical to remember is that it is that *first follower* who you are really trying to connect with and attract. This is not done through trickery or enticements. It has to be simple attraction that occurs naturally.

That *first follower* will need to be just as passionate and inspired as you are about what you are doing.

The *first follower* needs to be a highly visible and influential advocate. He or she needs to be your ultimate billboard who capably displays the payoff people will receive when they join your movement or buy your product or service. Think of that *first follower* as your PR/marketing person.

The *first follower* is the fulcrum that leverages your movement beyond your own inspiration and passion.

To recap: if you want to start a movement, you must first be fully engaged in your activity—to the point where you don't care how it is perceived. All you know is that it's cool, it's fun, and you want to keep doing it. It's selfish, but it's your life.

> *That first follower needs to be just as passionate and inspired as the leader.*

While attracting that elusive *first follower* is a big step forward, it is not your goal. Your goal is to make whatever you're doing more enjoyable and more beneficial for yourself, and possibly for others as well.

You can't manufacture a movement. You must be naturally passionate about what you are doing in order for it to be emotionally attractive to others. You can't fake passion for very long.

Remember, the *first follower* has to find you, not the other way around. What you have to do is recognize when he or she shows up!

If you're at all a creature of habit, and most of us are, you could easily get caught in the trap of waiting for the perfect conditions to occur.

## NEWS FLASH:
### The conditions will almost never be perfect!

Knowing and believing that perfect conditions may never occur will give you a tremendous head start with your movement. In the meantime, if you feel hesitant about any of your movement's components, consider the following suggestions as alternative or backup steps:

- If there is nothing *inspiring* you, start seriously looking for inspiration— in your work, in your hobbies, at home, and in your life. It's out there.

*Connect, associate, identify, and feel in harmony with your project, your movement, your passion.*

- If you feel you have no visibility, start seeking out visibility opportunities. Change your lens so you can more quickly spot and focus on ways to be more visible—join clubs, organizations, associations, other movements, or cool cliques to increase your chances of seeing the myriad of opportunities that are out there. In other words, you have to go to them; opportunities will almost never come to you.

- If you struggle with finding opportunities to share what you are doing, stop looking and begin to focus more on what you see as opportunities for you in your movement. That is, opportunities for you to have fun, to feel connected, to feel in the zone, or to feel like you're accomplishing something.

Once you're clear about your own opportunities, you can more easily show others how to connect the dots and see how they could plug into your movement.

Lastly, if there's no music for you to dance to (for your own magic dance), start humming to yourself. There is no point in identifying reasons not to start your movement. The majority of people talk themselves out of moving forward out of fear, frustration, or sometimes laziness. It's easier sometimes to just sit on the sidelines and judge everyone else.

Start your own music, keep playing it, and start dancing. And if you happen to hear someone else playing cool music, dance to that instead. It's simply a case of connecting. Connecting as in associating with, identifying with and feeling in harmony with your project, your movement, your passion.

Start humming.

# INSPIRATION

*Thoughts, Questions, and Actions*

## THOUGHTS

Inspiration can strike at any time.

The key is to recognize it when it comes along <u>and</u> to appreciate it just as quickly.

## QUESTIONS

Which people and things inspire you?

What precisely about them inspires you?

How do they inspire you into action?

## ACTIONS

Spend time consciously seeking to be inspired.

Hang around people you find inspiring as much as you can.

Never discount or underestimate the impact an inspiring person or circumstance can have on you. (In other words, appreciate it when you see it/feel it.)

Get into the habit of creating. Release yourself from the chains of judgment and criticism (by you and from others) by relentlessly creating, inventing, and working on things that you like.

# VISIBILITY

*Thoughts, Questions, and Actions*

## THOUGHTS

Visibility is a conscious action. It can happen accidentally, but when you are first starting a movement it is all about *who* sees you and *where* they see you. It's all about visibility.

## QUESTIONS

What are some of the obvious venues that will consistently increase your movement's visibility?

How can you increase your awareness of
visibility opportunities when they appear?

How can you stop those thoughts of doubt from creeping into your head and stopping you from becoming more visible?

## ACTIONS

Make yourself more aware of what feelings and/or situations prevent you from stepping out and being more visible.

Notice if it's shame, embarrassment, or a lack of self-confidence that's holding you back.

# OPPORTUNITY

*Thoughts, Questions, and Actions*

## THOUGHTS

Opportunities are everywhere, but this doesn't mean that you must act on every one that comes along. Discernment is essential.

## QUESTIONS

How do you know when a real opportunity has come along?

The three statements below will help you. If you can say Yes to all three, there is an increased likelihood that an opportunity exists.

1. This is something that I can see myself doing or being involved with 5 years from now. I feel this way because:

2. I feel it will be beneficial to me and
to others. I feel this way because:

3. I care enough about the opportunity to do it right, but I absolutely refuse to suffer because of it. I feel this way because:

## ACTIONS

Rather than being on the prowl for opportunities, shift your mindset to acute awareness of what inspires you.

Keep reminding yourself that inspiration creates opportunities, without effort.

# "MY MOVEMENT" PLANNING

The vision for my movement is:

The term *movement* can mean just that, or it could represent a project, a product, or a service.

I'm inspired (or not) because:

I'm visible (or not) because:

The opportunity is:

While the three major ingredients do lend themselves to the creation of a movement, there is still no guarantee that it will happen. By consciously reviewing and referring to the above steps, you increase the likelihood, and thus your chances, of success.

## What's Holding You Back?

There will likely be times when you think you *should* be ready to move forward, but you don't feel that way. Sometimes obvious things are missed because they are right in front of you. Consider the questions on the next few pages as a review of how you perceive your role as a leader.

## What's holding you back?

Is it you? (as in your fears, doubts, anxieties, or lack of confidence)

Is it because of others? (comments, judgments, criticisms, or just that look of disappointment)

What areas of your life do you gravitate towards, or where do you prefer to be? There are no wrong answers here.

As the leader: (at home, at work, in the community, in clubs, or at church?)

As a follower: (at home, at work, in the community, in clubs, or at church?)

When was the last time you were a *first follower*? Was it a conscious decision? What were the results? Would you do it again?

# ACKNOWLEDGEMENTS

I have had many opportunities to lead, to follow, to get out of the way, and to be a *first follower*. Each one was an enjoyable experience. So unless you or the person you are following is dishonest, hurtful, or fear-inducing, your experiences should be enjoyable ones, too.

My thanks to the following individuals for their input and guidance, and for modeling great leadership: Bill Bennett, Rick Wright, David Baker, Jill and Dave Luhrsen, and Ann McNeill.

A big *thank you* to Derek Sivers for allowing me to run with his concept of the *first follower*. Your generosity is much appreciated.

And thanks once again to Maura and Vanessa for their feedback and support.

Jeff Pasquale is an executive and life coach who works specifically in the areas of life, leadership, and legacy. He is the author of **How BIG is Your Target** – The Power of Focus in a Cluttered World, **Looking for SUNSHINE** — A Practical Guide for Dealing with Life's Challenges, **Subway Life** – An Underground Guide to Balanced Living, **Get That New Job**, and **Coaching Leadership** – If Not You, Who?

He lives in Boynton Beach, Florida.

More information about Jeff and additional tools can be found at:

www.JeffPasquale.com

**NOTES:**

NOTES:

**NOTES:**

**NOTES:**

**NOTES:**

www.ingramcontent.com/pod-product-compliance
Lightning Source LLC
Chambersburg PA
CBHW060118050426
42448CB00010B/1918